Editor
Lorin E. Klistoff, M.A.

Managing Editor
Karen Goldfluss, M.S. Ed.

Editor-in-Chief
Sharon Coan, M.S. Ed.

Illustrator
Becky Radtke

Cover Artist
Brenda DiAntonis

Art Director
CJae Froshay

Imaging
James Edward Grace

Product Manager
Phil Garcia

Product Developer
Quack & Co.

Publishers
Rachelle Cracchiolo, M.S. Ed.
Mary Dupuy Smith, M.S. Ed.

John 3:16

Author

Becky Radtke

Teacher Created Materials, Inc.
6421 Industry Way
Westminster, CA 92683
www.teachercreated.com
ISBN-0-7439-7100-0
©2002 Teacher Created Materials, Inc.
Reprinted, 2003
Made in U.S.A.

Table of Contents

Introduction 3
Creation 4
    All the Animals 5
    Adam and Eve 6
    The Garden of Eden 7
    A Bounty of Food 8
    Adam and Eve Sin 9
    Time to Go 10
Noah and the Ark 11
    Awesome Animals 12
    It's Raining! It's Pouring! 13
    God's Promise 14
The Tower of Babel 15
    God Got Angry 16
    What Did You Say? 17
    Let's Move Away 18
Abraham and Sarah 19
    A Wonderful Son 20
    A Great Girl 21
    Two Baby Boys 22
Joseph and the Colorful Coat 23
    Angry Brothers 24
    Hungry Brothers 25
    Joseph Is Kind 26
Samson and Delilah 27
    A Hairy Story 28
    To the Temple 29
    God Helps Samson 30
Naomi and Ruth 31
    Working for Food 32
    A Nice Couple 33
    Grandma Naomi 34
Samuel Gets Called 35
    Listen, Samuel 36
    Who's Calling? 37
    A Special Message 38
David, the Next King 39
    Nice to Meet You 40
    Eight in All 41
    David Is Chosen 42
David and Goliath 43
    David Is Brave 44
    Watch Out, Goliath! 45
    David Defeats Goliath 46
King Josiah 47
    Finding God's Law 48
    Josiah Listens to God 49
    Time to Celebrate! 50
Queen Esther 51
    Mean Old Haman 52
    Please, Save Us! 53
    God Save the Queen! 54
A Furnace of Fire 55
    Wow! That's Hot! 56
    Getting Out Alive 57
    Worship the One True God 58
Daniel and the Lions 59
    A New Rule 60
    Daniel's in Trouble 61
    Daniel Is Safe 62
Jonah and the Big Fish 63
    A Super Storm 64
    Inside a Fish 65
    Jonah Obeys God 66
Mary, the Mother of Jesus 67
    A Special Visit 68
    A Sweet Little Baby 69
    Mary and an Angel 70
A Baby for Elizabeth 71
A Happy Baby 72
    It's a Boy! 73
    A Special Name 74
Jesus Is Born 75
    A Crowded City 76
    Staying in a Stable 77
    God's Son Is Born 78
Shepherds and Jesus 79
    Look! A Light! 80
    What Good News! 81
    Look What We Found! 82
Jesus Is Blessed 83
    Holy Simeon 84
    Simeon's Savior 85
    Anna Thanks God 86
Wise Men Visit 87
    Where Is He? 88
    See the Star? 89
    Let's Go Home! 90
Jesus at the Temple 91
    Where Is Jesus? 92
    Such a Smart Boy! 93
    Don't Worry 94
Jesus Is Baptized 95
    Confess and Be Baptized 96
    Please Baptize Me 97
    God Loves His Son 98
Jesus Picks Disciples 99
    Come, Follow Me 100
    Matthew's New Job 101
    Twelve Special Men 102
A Wedding Feast 103
    It's a Miracle! 104
    Last but Not Least 105
    The First of Many 106
Jesus Calms the Storm 107
    What a Storm! 108
    Help! Jesus, Help! 109
    Be Still! 110
A Girl Lives 111
    Is It Too Late? 112
    Jesus Knows 113
    A Happy Day 114
Fish and Loaves 115
    A Busy Day 116
    A Little for a Lot 117
    Food for All 118
Jesus Walks on Water 119
    Windy and Weary 120
    A Special Walk 121
    Peter Tries It, Too 122
A Good Samaritan 123
    Who Will Help? 124
    A Kind Man 125
    Be Kind to Everyone 126
Prodigal Son 127
    Party Time 128
    A Dirty Job 129
    A Happy Homecoming 130
Jesus Rides Through Jerusalem 131
    Look Who's Coming 132
    All Through the Town 133
Jesus Dies and Rises Up 134
    He Did Nothing Wrong 135
    A Cross to Bear 136
    Accept This Gift 137
    Jesus Rises Up 138
    Jesus Is Alive! 139
Answer Key 140

Introduction

What an exciting way for young children to learn some wonderful Bible stories! This book is filled with stimulating puzzles and activities children can complete to learn all about Creation, Noah, David, Josiah, Daniel, the life and death of Christ, and much more.

Children will have a great time as they work mazes, color pictures, decode messages, follow directions, complete crossword puzzles, solve math problems, and more—all while learning the Bible.

This book is a perfect tool for teachers in Christian schools, Sunday school teachers, parents, and any other adults wanting to help children learn about God. Each Bible story featured covers several pages, so you might want to spend several days on each one. Read the contents of each page to your child, and go over the directions with him or her. Be sure to help your children with each activity to ensure understanding.

After each story is finished, discuss it with your child. Help your child come to better understand the Bible and God's great love for us.

Regardless of how this book is used, all children will enjoy the wonderful Bible stories and exciting activities it has to offer!

Creation

(Genesis 1–2)

God created everything on the earth and in heaven.
Connect the dots to see what God made to light the sky
each day!

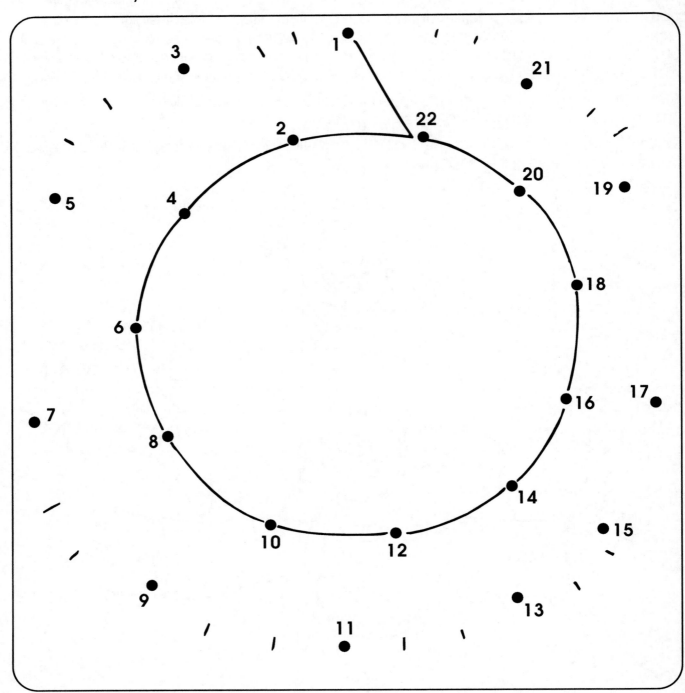

All the Animals

(Genesis 1)

The Lord created all the animals in our world. He made them large and small.

Count how many times the duck says "quack." Write this number on the tree stump.

Adam and Eve

(Genesis 1–2)

God made the first man and woman. The man's name was Adam. The woman's name was Eve.

Circle **Adam** and **Eve** in the puzzle. The names may go across or down. Write the number of times "Adam" was circled on the tree. Write the number of times "Eve" was circled on the bush.

The Garden of Eden

(Genesis 2)

Adam and Eve lived in a beautiful place God made. It was called the Garden of Eden. This garden was full of beautiful plants and flowers. It was full of many good things to eat.

Help Adam and Eve find their way to the pretty flowers.

A Bounty of Food

(Genesis 2)

The Garden of Eden was filled with lots of delicious food for Adam and Eve to eat.

Color each food the same color as the crayon below it.

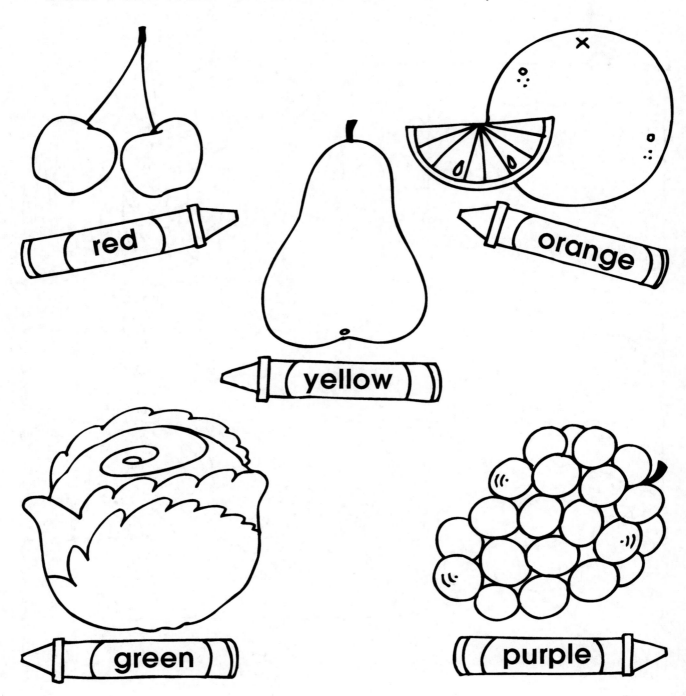

Adam and Eve Sin

(Genesis 3)

God told Adam and Eve never to eat the fruit from a certain tree in their special garden. One day, a serpent tempted Eve to eat some of the fruit. Eve and Adam ate the fruit. Now they had disobeyed God. They had sinned.

Look at the picture below. Find and circle the 5 hidden fruits.

Time to Go

(Genesis 3)

Because they sinned, God told Adam and Eve they had to leave the wonderful Garden of Eden. How sad they must have been!

Find and color these shapes in the picture below.

Noah and the Ark

(Genesis 6–9)

God saw how evil people on the earth had become. God was sad. He told the only good man he could find that He was going to send a terrible flood. This man was named Noah. God wanted Noah to build something to keep him and his family safe.

To find out what it was, connect the dots.

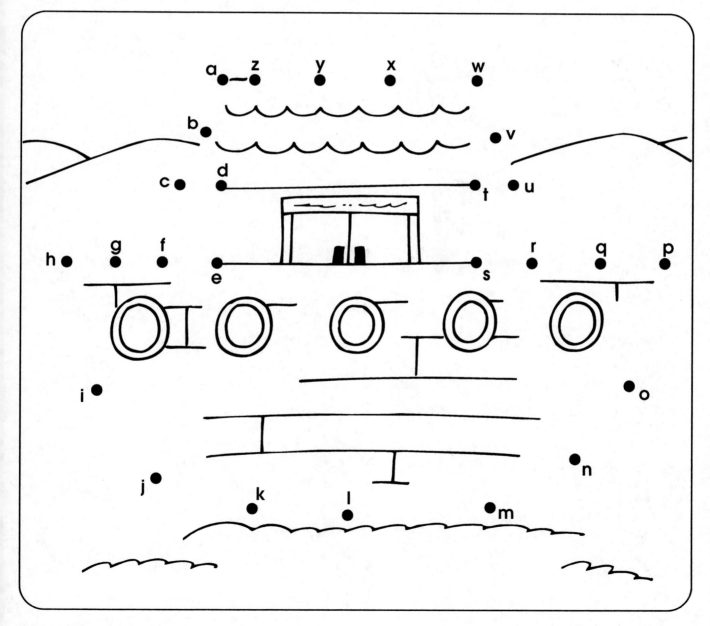

Awesome Animals

(Genesis 6–9)

God told Noah how to build a huge boat. Then He told Noah to bring pairs of every kind of animal onto the boat.

Have you seen all these animals at the zoo? Match each animal to its outline.

It's Raining! It's Pouring!

(Genesis 6–9)

It took a long time for Noah to build the ark. When it was done, Noah, his family, and all the animals went on board. Then God made the rain fall. It rained and rained for forty days and nights.

Color all the big raindrops green. Color all the small raindrops blue.

God's Promise

(Genesis 6–9)

The ark kept Noah, his family, and the animals safe from the flood. Finally, the rain stopped. There was dry land again. Then God told Noah they could all leave the ark. God put something in the sky as a sign of His promise to never destroy all living creatures again.

To find out what it is, write each letter in the matching numbered blank.

Abraham and Sarah

(Genesis 15)

God told Abraham that he would someday have as many family members as there were stars in the sky.

Find 5 stars below. Color them yellow.

A Wonderful Son

(Genesis 21)

As He promised, God blessed Abraham and Sarah with a son. His name was Isaac.

Use the code to color the picture of this happy family.

1 = yellow

2 = pink

4 = green

3 = gray

5 = brown

6 = blue

A Great Girl

(Genesis 24)

Isaac grew to be a man. One day, a servant went out to find him a wife. The servant found a wonderful girl named Rebekah.

Use the clues to find which girl is Rebekah.

1. She is smiling.
2. She is holding a water jug.
3. She has bracelets on her wrists.
4. She has a striped robe on.

A   B   C   D

Two Baby Boys

(Genesis 25)

Isaac loved Rebekah very much. They got married. They had two boys named Esau and Jacob.

Draw a line to connect the two brothers that look exactly the same.

Samson and Delilah

(Judges 16)

Samson was a very strong man. Some Philistine rulers wanted Delilah to find out what made Samson so strong.

To discover what the rulers said they would pay her, color every coin that has a capital letter on it. Then write each of those letters, in order, on the lines below.

_____ _____ _____ _____ _____ _____

A Hairy Story

(Judges 16)

Delilah kept asking Samson what made him so strong. At first, Samson lied. Finally, he told Delilah the truth.

Cross out all the letters **a**, **b**, and **d**. The letters that are left spell out what needed to be done to Samson's long hair to make him weak. Write the letters in order on the lines below.

b	a	d	b	d
d	c	b	d	a
a	d	a	u	d
a	b	d	b	d
t	b	d	a	b

_____ _____ _____

To the Temple

(Judges 16)

Samson told Delilah that if his hair was cut, he would not be strong. When Samson fell asleep, a Philistine cut his hair. Now Samson was weak. Some men put him in prison. After awhile, some Philistine people wanted to make fun of Samson at the temple.

Use a crayon to trace over the correct path that will take Samson to the temple.

God Helps Samson

(Judges 16)

Samson was taken from prison to the temple. The people there planned to make fun of Samson. Samson prayed. With God's help, Samson pushed over something that destroyed the temple and all the people.

Connect the dots to find out what Samson pushed over.

Samuel Gets Called

(1 Samuel 1)

Young Samuel came to live with Eli, the priest. Eli taught Samuel to obey God.

Connect the dots.

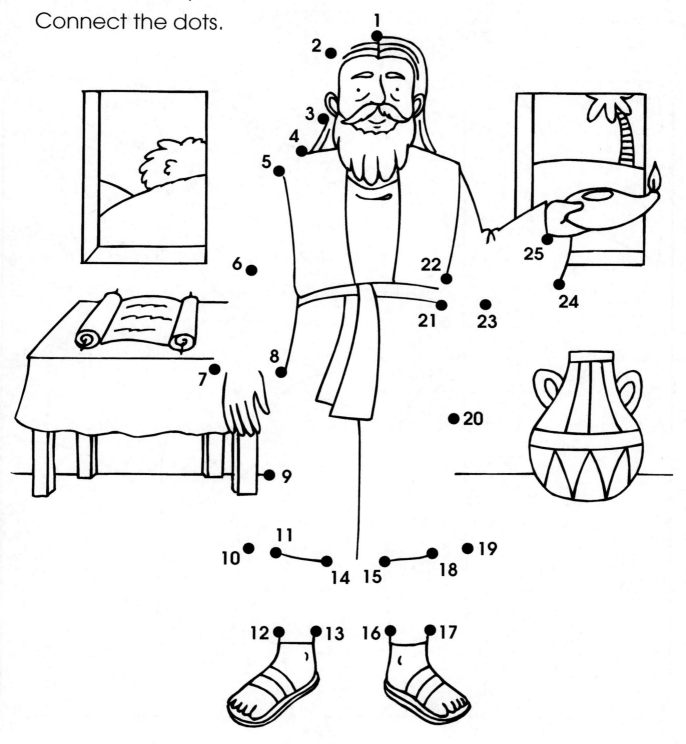

Listen, Samuel

(1 Samuel 3)

One night, young Samuel thought Eli was calling to him. To find out how many times Samuel heard his name called, color every space with a **number** yellow. Color every space with a **letter** green.

Who's Calling?

(1 Samuel 3)

Eli told Samuel that he had not called to him. To find out who called to Samuel, write the word name of each picture. The letters in the boxes will spell who really called him.

A Special Message

(1 Samuel 3)

Eli told Samuel that the Lord was calling to him. So when God called again, Samuel was ready to listen. God told Samuel a message.

Help Samuel go tell Eli the message. Follow the letters that spell **Samuel**.

David, the Next King

(1 Samuel 16)

Young Samuel grew to be a prophet. One day, God sent Samuel to see a man named Jesse. God had chosen one of Jesse's sons to be the next king.

Use the grid to draw the other half of his crown.

Nice to Meet You

(1 Samuel 16)

Samuel met seven of Jesse's sons.

Look up and down and across in the tent for the word **seven**. Write how many times you find it in the circle at the bottom.

```
n  v  e  n  s  e  s  v  s
e  s  e  s  e  v  e  n  e
v  e  s  e  v  e  n  e  v
e  v  e  v  e  s  n  v  e
s  e  v  e  n  e  v  e  n
e  n  s  v  e  n  s  s  e
v  e  s  e  v  e  n  e  v
```

Eight in All

(1 Samuel 16)

After meeting seven of Jesse's sons, Samuel asked Jesse if he had any more. Jesse had one more son named David.

Connect the dots to see what David watched over.

David Is Chosen

(1 Samuel 16)

God told Samuel that He wanted Jesse's youngest son to be the next king. His name was David. So Samuel put holy oil on David.

Which of the pieces below will finish this picture? Color it.

David and Goliath

(1 Samuel 17)

The Philistines and the Israelite people were ready to battle each other. One of the Philistine soldiers was a huge man.

To find out his name, put the helmets in the correct order.

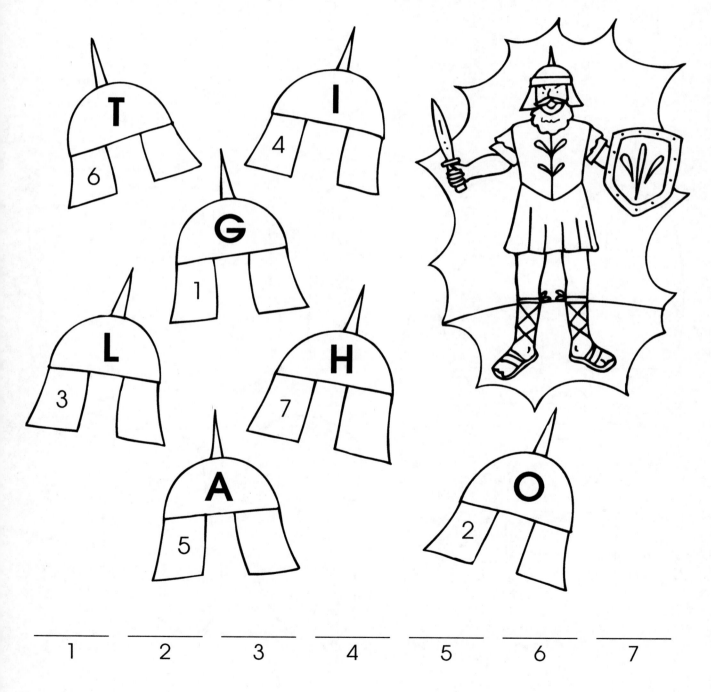

____ ____ ____ ____ ____ ____ ____

  1   2   3   4   5   6   7

David Is Brave

(1 Samuel 17)

Young David was not a soldier. Yet, David wanted to fight the mighty Goliath. To do this, David took 5 smooth stones.

Solve the math problem on each stone. Then use the code to find out what David wanted to put the stones in.

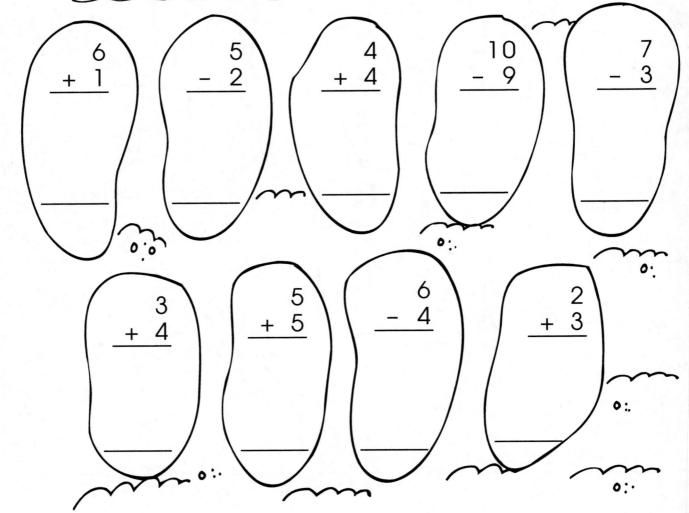

1 = N	3 = L	5 = T	8 = I
2 = O	4 = G	7 = S	10 = H

$$\begin{array}{r} 6 \\ +\ 1 \\ \hline \end{array}$$

$$\begin{array}{r} 5 \\ -\ 2 \\ \hline \end{array}$$

$$\begin{array}{r} 4 \\ +\ 4 \\ \hline \end{array}$$

$$\begin{array}{r} 10 \\ -\ 9 \\ \hline \end{array}$$

$$\begin{array}{r} 7 \\ -\ 3 \\ \hline \end{array}$$

$$\begin{array}{r} 3 \\ +\ 4 \\ \hline \end{array}$$

$$\begin{array}{r} 5 \\ +\ 5 \\ \hline \end{array}$$

$$\begin{array}{r} 6 \\ -\ 4 \\ \hline \end{array}$$

$$\begin{array}{r} 2 \\ +\ 3 \\ \hline \end{array}$$

Watch Out, Goliath!

(1 Samuel 17)

David put a stone in his slingshot. He whirled it around. The stone flew right at the giant!

Find six things that are in the top picture but are not in the bottom picture.

David Defeats Goliath

(1 Samuel 17)

David's stone hit Goliath right in the forehead! Mighty Goliath fell down. God helped David defeat the huge giant!

Cross out the letter **M** and every other letter after it. Then write the letters that are left in order. This is what David's side yelled.

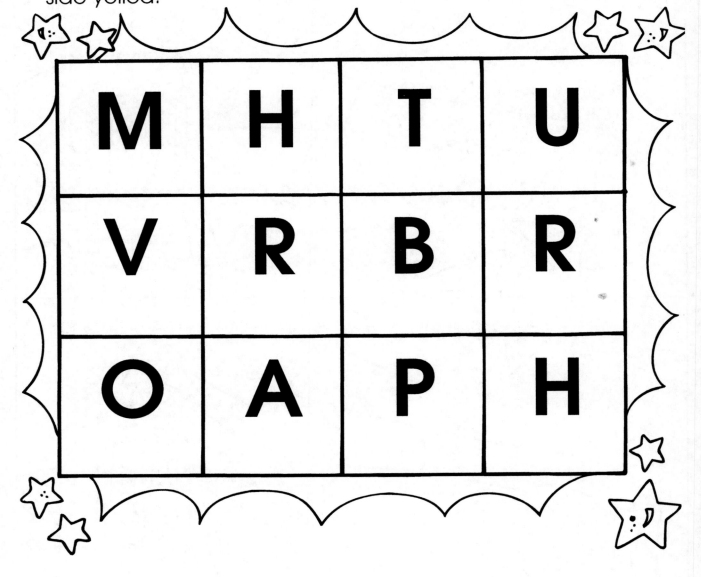

M	H	T	U
V	R	B	R
O	A	P	H

___ ___ ___ ___   ___ ___ ___ ___

King Josiah

(2 Kings 22)

Josiah was only eight years old when he became the king of Judah. When Josiah became a man, he ordered that the temple be fixed up. While work was being done, a priest found an important scroll.

Help Josiah choose the right path to find the scroll.

Finding God's Law

(2 Kings 22–23)

God's law was written on the scroll. When it was read to King Josiah, he became very sad. Josiah and his people weren't living as God wanted them to.

Find the shapes in the picture. Color them yellow.

Queen Esther

(Esther 2)

King Xerxes was looking for a wife. He chose a beautiful girl named Esther. He did not know Esther and her Uncle Mordecai were Jews.

Draw a square around the picture of Esther that is different from the others.

Mean Old Haman

(Esther 3)

Esther's uncle, Mordecai, refused to do something. It made Haman so angry that he got the king to agree that all Jewish people should be killed. This meant Uncle Mordecai and Esther, too. The king had no idea these two were Jewish.

Start at the "H" and follow the arrows to find what Mordecai wouldn't do. Write the letters in order on the blanks.

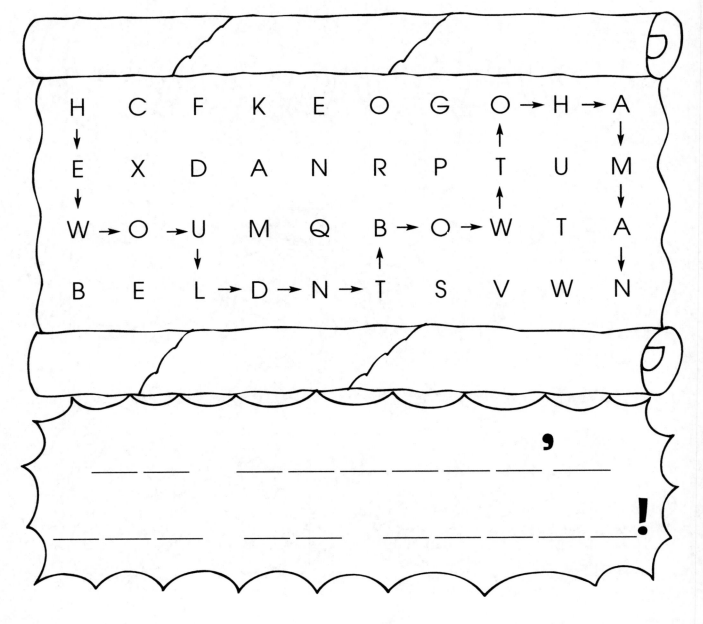

Please, Save Us!

(Esther 7)

Queen Esther went to the king. She told him she was Jewish.
Esther asked him to save her and her people.

Color the picture using the code.

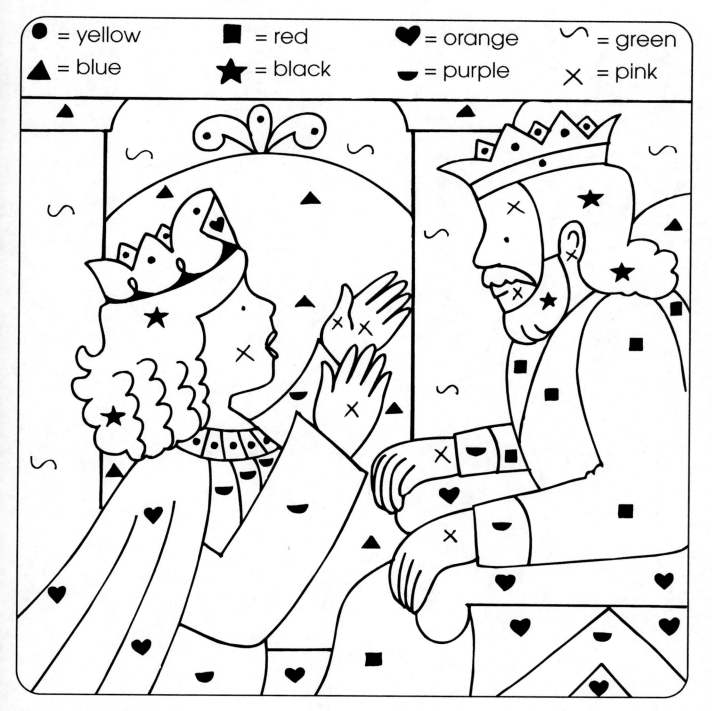

God Save the Queen!

(Esther 7–8)

Queen Esther saved the Jewish people!

Color the crowns that contain all the letters needed to spell **Queen Esther**.

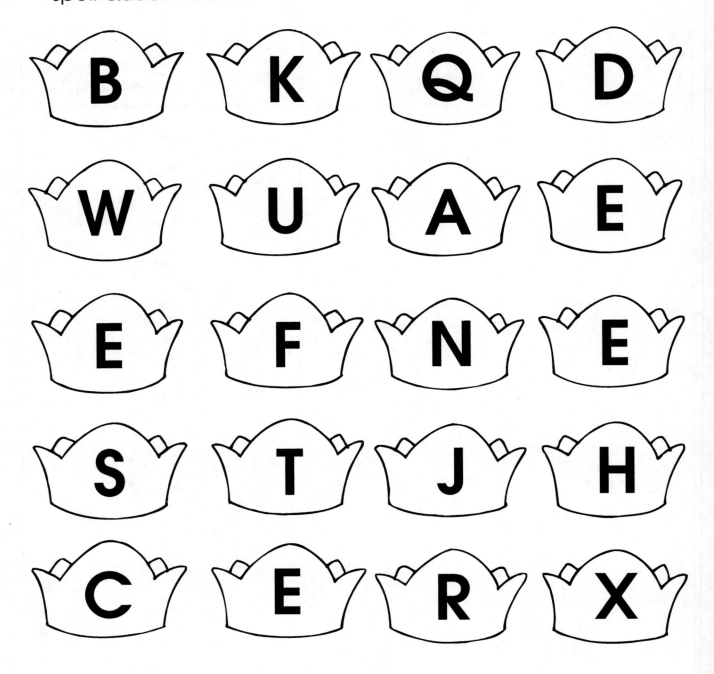

Bible Brain Teasers

Daniel and the Lions

(Daniel 6)

King Darius gave Daniel an important job in his kingdom. This made some other workers very angry.

To find out what the workers wanted Daniel to get into, cross out all letters **K**, **N**, and **I**. Write the letters that are left, in order, on the lines.

N	I	L	K	I	N	O	I	I	N	K	I	K	N
K	I	N	I	K	T	K	N	K	I	K	I	K	I
I	N	I	S	I	N	I	N	I	N	I	N	N	
K	I	K	I	K	I	N	K	N	N	K	I	K	I
N	I	N	K	N	O	I	N	K	K	I	N	I	N
I	K	I	K	I	K	F	I	N	I	T	I	R	I
I	N	N	I	N	N	K	N	I	N	K	N	K	N
K	I	O	I	K	K	U	I	K	B	I	I	I	K
L	K	N	K	N	N	N	I	N	I	N	K	E	N	N

_____ _____ _____ _____ _____ _____ _____ _____ _____ _____ _____ _____

_____ _____ _____ _____ _____ _____ _____ _____ _____ _____ _____ **!**

A New Rule

(Daniel 6)

The jealous workers talked King Darius into making a new rule: Everyone was to pray only to the king. Daniel didn't follow this rule. He kept praying to God.

Look at the picture below carefully. Find and color these hidden objects: cup, pencil, heart, and boot.

Daniel's in Trouble

(Daniel 6)

King Darius liked Daniel. He was sad that he had to punish Daniel for praying to God. The king ordered that Daniel be thrown into a den of lions.

How many lion shapes are here? Write that number on the lion's den.

Daniel Is Safe

(Daniel 6)

Daniel was thrown into the lions' den. When King Darius checked on him the next day, Daniel was fine! God had sent an angel to protect him. The king was glad. He had Daniel brought out of the den.

Read the directions. Color the dots to get Daniel to the word **FREE**.

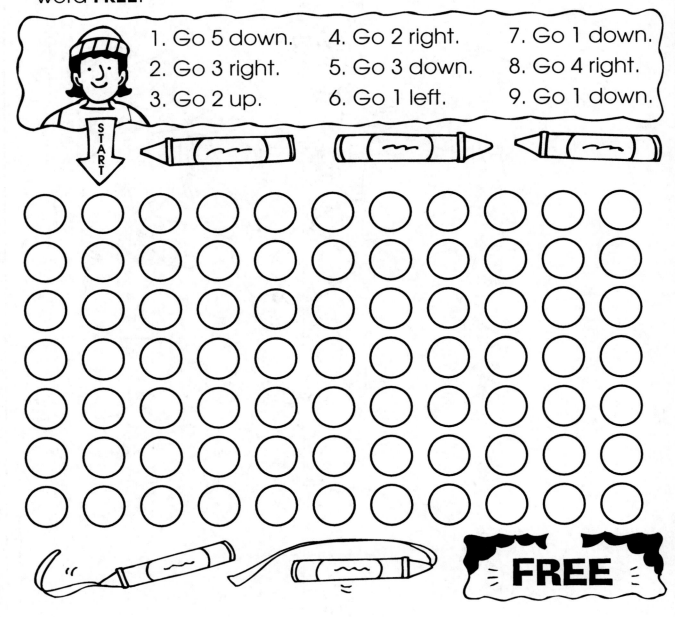

1. Go 5 down.
2. Go 3 right.
3. Go 2 up.
4. Go 2 right.
5. Go 3 down.
6. Go 1 left.
7. Go 1 down.
8. Go 4 right.
9. Go 1 down.

START

FREE

Inside a Fish

(Jonah 1–2)

The sailors tossed Jonah into the ocean so the terrible storm would end. A huge fish swallowed Jonah. Inside the fish, Jonah prayed to God.

Color all the big fish green. Color all the small fish orange.

Jonah Obeys God

(Jonah 3)

Inside the big fish, Jonah asked God to save him. The fish spit Jonah out on the shore. Then Jonah obeyed God. He went to the city of Nineveh. He warned the people to stop sinning.

Color the path from 1 to 20 to get Jonah to Nineveh.

2	18	19	20	
16	17	7		
15	14	13	19	15	8
8	17	12	11	10	9
		8	16	7	8
	1	6	14	6	13
	2	3	4	5	9

Nineveh

Mary, the Mother of Jesus

(Luke 1)

In Nazareth, Mary was engaged to marry Joseph.
Write the missing numbers in the trail of rings.

A Special Visit

(Luke 1)

One day, something very special happened to Mary. She had a visitor who told her not to be afraid.

Connect the dots to see who this visitor was.

A Sweet Little Baby

(Luke 1)

An angel told young Mary that she was going to have God's very own son! She was to call the baby Jesus.

Find and color these hidden baby objects:

bottle   diaper   crib   blanket   rattle

Mary and an Angel

(Luke 1)

Mary told the angel that she would obey God. She was going to be the mother of baby Jesus.

To find out the name of the angel who visited Mary, write the first letter of each picture in the blanks.

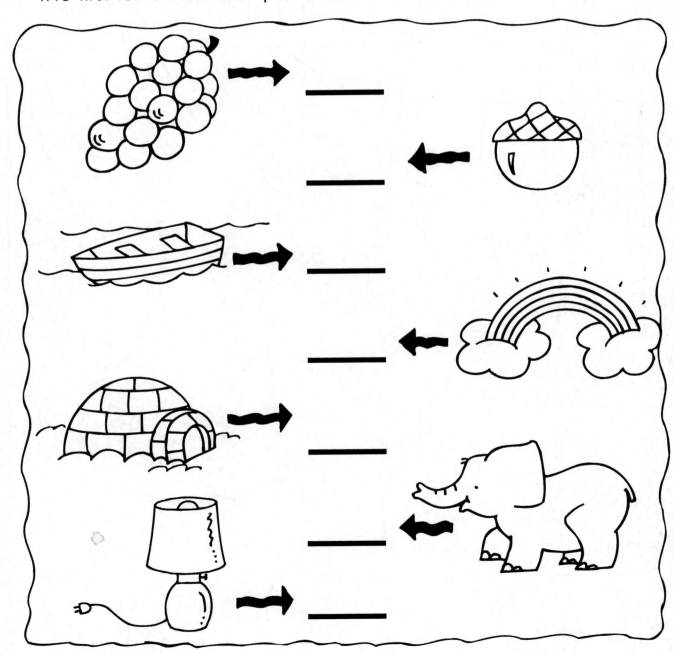

70

A Baby for Elizabeth

(Luke 1)

Mary went to visit her cousin Elizabeth. They were both going to have babies.

Color the path of triangles to help Mary get to Elizabeth.

A Happy Baby

(Luke 1)

Elizabeth learned that Mary was going to be the mother of God's son. Elizabeth's baby did something when it heard Mary's voice.

Cross out the first bottle and every other one after that. Then write the remaining letters in order onto the blanks to spell what the baby did.

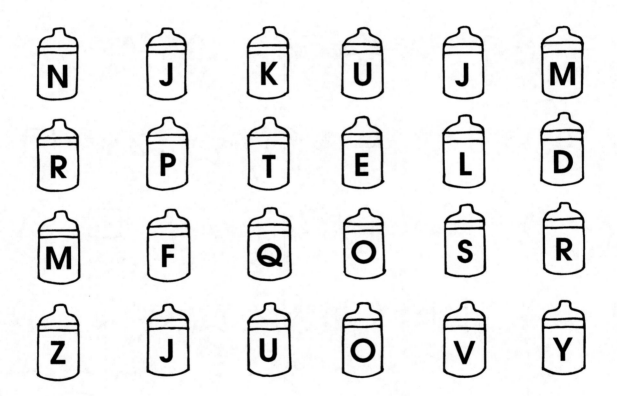

___ ___ ___ ___ ___ ___

___ ___ ___ ___ ___ ___!

It's a Boy!

(Luke 1)

Soon after Mary left, Elizabeth had a baby boy. Her family thought he should be named Zechariah, like his father. Zechariah had been unable to speak for almost a year.

Finish drawing the top picture so it looks like the bottom one.

A Special Name

(Luke 1)

An angel came to Zechariah. He told him what his baby's name should be. Since Zechariah could not speak, he wrote the name down on a piece of paper. Soon after he did this, Zechariah was able to speak again!

Use the code to find out what Zechariah wanted to name the baby.

▲ = blue   ● = yellow

Jesus Is Born

(Matthew 1, Luke 1–2)

Joseph was engaged to a young woman named Mary. An angel told Joseph that Mary was going to have God's son. Joseph and Mary became husband and wife. Then they had to travel to Joseph's home town to be counted.

To find the name of the town they went to, follow the directions.

Write the letter **e** in each star.

Write the letter **m** inside the square.

Write a capital **B** in the circle.

Write the letter **l** in the triangle.

Write the letter **h** in the heart.

A Crowded City

(Luke 2)

Mary and Joseph went to Bethlehem. When they got there, it was very crowded. They couldn't find a place to stay.

Count each group of people. Write the number in the arrow.

Staying in a Stable

(Luke 2)

When they got to Bethlehem, Joseph and Mary needed to find a place to sleep. But all the inns were full. They stayed in a stable that was used to keep animals.

Unscramble the name of each picture shown.

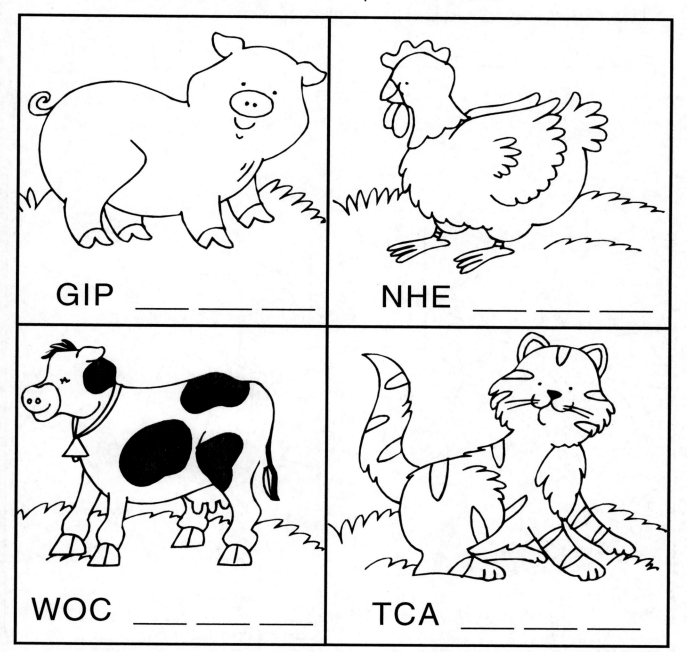

GIP ___ ___ ___

NHE ___ ___ ___

WOC ___ ___ ___

TCA ___ ___ ___

God's Son Is Born

(Luke 2)

Mary and Joseph decided to stay in a stable. During the night, a wonderful thing happened! Mary gave birth to Jesus—God's own son. She wrapped Him in a cloth and placed Him in a manger.

Use the code to color the picture.

1 = yellow   3 = brown   5 = blue

2 = black   4 = red   6 = purple

Shepherds and Jesus

(Luke 2)

The night Jesus was born, some shepherds were watching their sheep.

Find 5 sheep below. Color them gray.

79

Look! A Light!

(Luke 2)

Suddenly, the shepherds saw a bright light. An angel appeared to them!

To find out how the shepherds felt, write each letter in the matching numbered blank.

R 3   A 1   I 5

A 4   D 6   F 2

___ ___ ___ ___ ___ ___
 1   2   3   4   5   6

What Good News!

(Luke 2)

An angel told the shepherds some good news—a Savior had been born in Bethlehem! They could find the baby in a manger. The angels offered praises to God.

How many angels do you see? Color the correct number.

Look What We Found!

(Luke 2)

The shepherds went to Bethlehem. They found Mary, Joseph, and baby Jesus. They were so happy to see the new baby!

Find these words inside the stable. Look up, down, across, and diagonally.

MARY   JESUS   SHEPHERDS

BETHLEHEM   JOSEPH   HAPPY

B	T	P	R	S	H	E	P	H	E	R	D	S
Q	U	A	J	X	V	Z	W	N	X	V	U	G
Y	S	B	E	T	H	L	E	H	E	M	T	F
H	R	A	S	M	Z	S	B	L	H	W	E	H
O	A	N	U	K	R	F	Z	Y	A	M	Y	P
S	Z	P	S	E	Y	X	Y	L	I	N	I	E
B	Q	J	P	O	C	R	D	J	O	K	H	S
W	T	D	V	Y	A	X	K	B	N	I	S	O
U	C	P	W	M	Q	L	P	M	C	J	B	J

Jesus Is Blessed

(Luke 2:21–40)

Soon after the baby Jesus was born, Mary and Joseph took Him to Jerusalem. They were going to present Him to God. Find the path that will lead them to the temple.

Holy Simeon

(Luke 2)

Simeon lived a holy life. God told Simeon that he would see the Messiah before he died. Simeon was already at the temple when Mary, Joseph, and Jesus went inside.

Find the letters that spell **Simeon**. Color them orange.

Simeon's Savior

(Luke 2)

Simeon knew that Jesus was the Savior God had promised. He held baby Jesus. He thanked God for letting him see the child. Then Simeon did something to Mary, Joseph, and Jesus.

To find out what Simeon did, write the beginning letter of each picture in the blank.

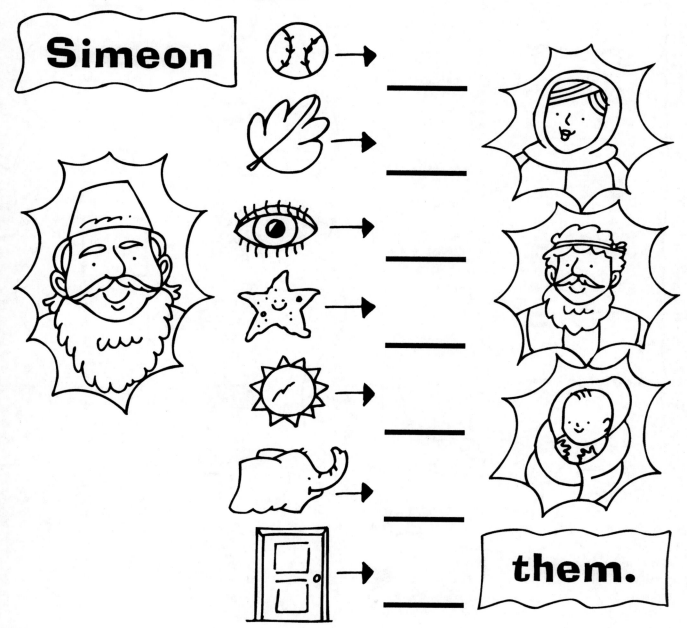

Anna Thanks God

(Luke 2)

Anna was a very old prophetess. She was at the temple when baby Jesus was there. Like Simeon, she thanked God that she was able to see Jesus. Anna told everyone that Jesus was special.

To find out what it was, use the code.

Wise Men Visit

(Matthew 2)

Some wise men heard about Jesus' birth. They traveled to Jerusalem and looked for Him. But baby Jesus wasn't there.

Color the picture using the code.

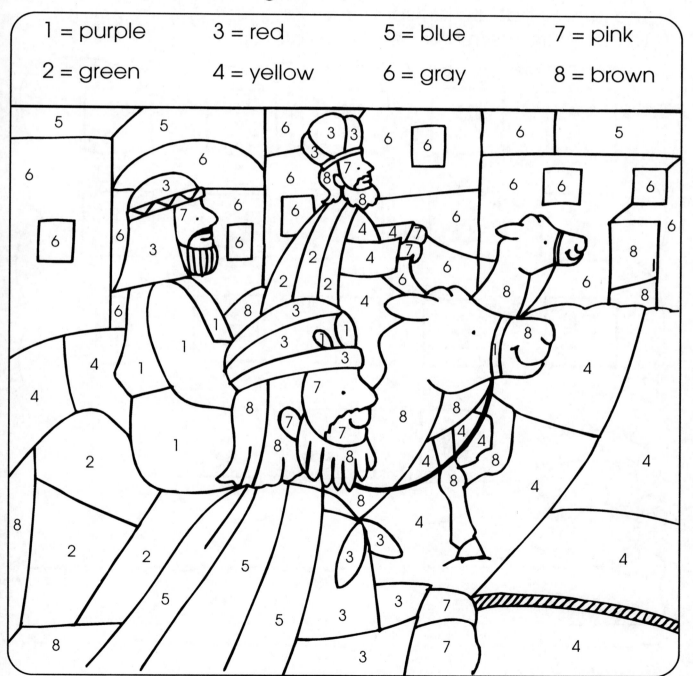

1 = purple	3 = red	5 = blue	7 = pink
2 = green	4 = yellow	6 = gray	8 = brown

Where Is He?

(Matthew 2)

King Herod pretended he wanted to find baby Jesus and worship Him. He asked the wise men to come back and tell him where Jesus was.

Cross out the first square and every other square after that. The letters that are left spell what King Herod really wanted to do. Write them in order on the blanks.

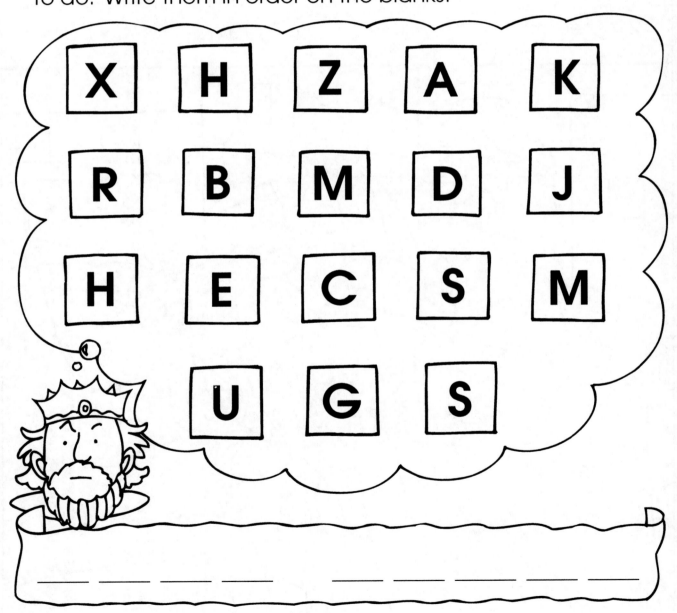

See the Star?

(Matthew 2)

The wise men followed a special star. It brought them to Jesus' home. They gave baby Jesus gifts of gold, frankincense, and myrrh.

Complete the maze to show the path the wise men took to see Jesus.

Let's Go Home!

(Luke 2)

In a dream, the wise men were warned not to tell King Herod where Jesus was. So they traveled home a different way.

Connect the dots to see what they may have ridden to get home.

Jesus at the Temple

(Luke 2)

Jesus grew and grew. When He was twelve, Mary and Joseph took Him to Jerusalem for Passover.

Circle the cakes that have twelve candles. Cross out the ones that do not.

Where Is Jesus?

(Luke 2)

On the way back to Jerusalem, Mary and Joseph couldn't find Jesus. He wasn't with anyone in their group.

Find and circle the name **Jesus** six times. Look up, down, and across.

```
S  J  E  S  U  S
E  E  U  J  S  U
U  S  J  E  S  E
J  S  U  J  J  E  S  U  S
S  S  E  U  E  J  U  S  J
U  J  E  J  S  U  S  J  E
S  J  E  S  U  S
E  S  U  E  S  S
J  U  J  S  J  U
```

Such a Smart Boy!

(Luke 2)

Mary and Joseph went back to Jerusalem to look for Jesus. At last, they found Him in the temple. He was talking with teachers and wise men. They were amazed at all Jesus knew!

Color the letters in alphabetical order to take Mary and Joseph to Jesus.

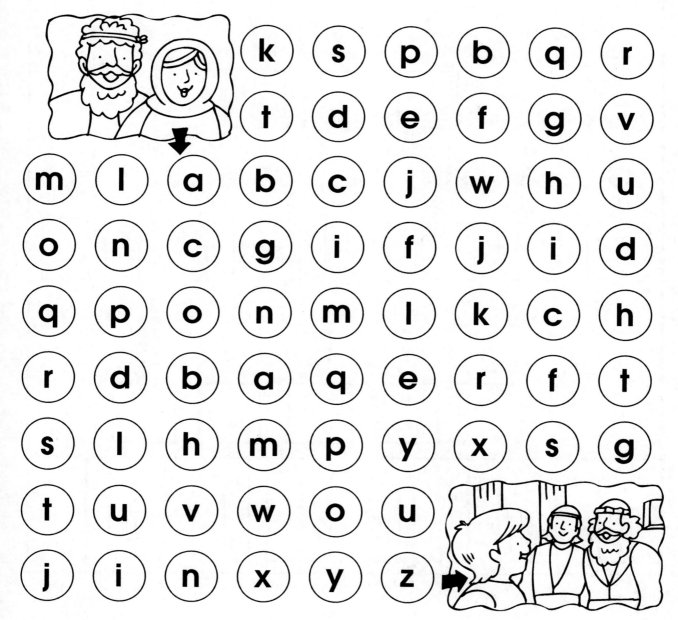

Don't Worry

(Luke 2)

Jesus didn't understand why Mary and Joseph had been worried about Him. He thought they knew where He was.

What did Jesus call the temple? Write the letter that comes before to find the answer.

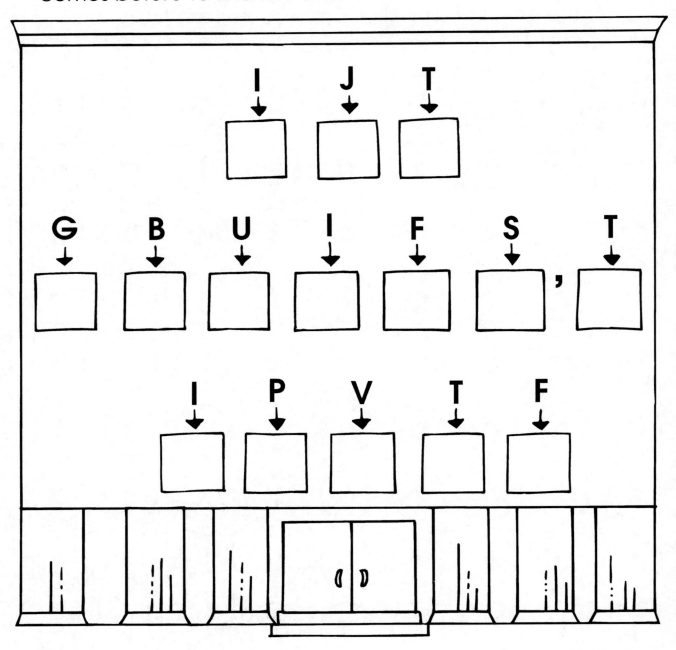

Jesus Picks Disciples

(Luke 5)

Jesus went on a boat with a fisherman named Peter. Jesus told him to drop the nets in the water. When they pulled them up, they were filled with fish.

Color the two fish in the net that look the same.

Come, Follow Me

(Luke 5)

Peter, Andrew, James, and John were fishermen who decided to follow Jesus.

To finish what Jesus said to them, write the words from the boats in order.

6 **catch**

3 **on**

5 **will**

7 **men**

4 **you**

1 **From**

2 **now**

_____ _____ _____ _____
  1   2   3   4

_____ _____ _____ .
  5   6   7

Matthew's New Job

(Luke 5)

Matthew was a tax collector. People didn't trust him. When Jesus asked Matthew to follow Him, he did!

Match each tax collector to the right number of coins.

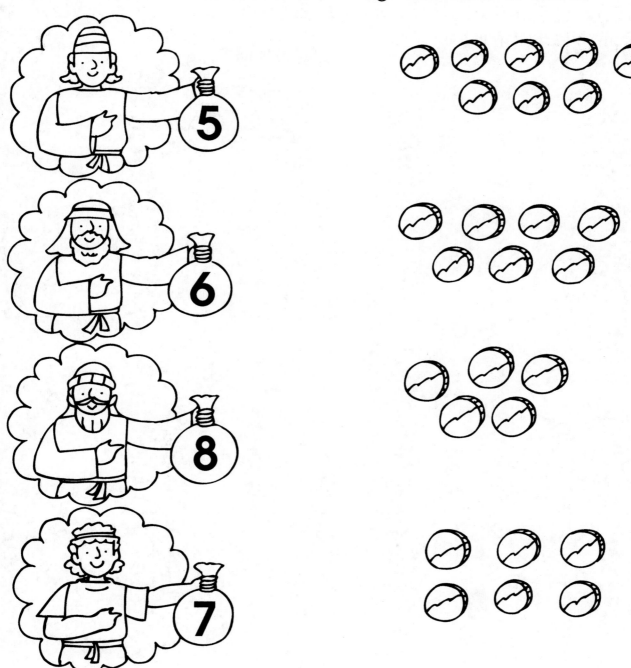

Twelve Special Men

(Luke 5–6)

Jesus chose twelve men to be His disciples. Their names were Peter, Andrew, James, John, Philip, Bartholomew, Thomas, Matthew, James, Thaddaeus, Simon, and Judas.

Use a different colored crayon to lightly color each name in the letter trail.

A Wedding Feast

(John 2)

Jesus, His mother, and the twelve disciples were invited to a wedding. At the wedding, Mary saw something that was all gone.

Unscramble the letters in the glasses to see what was all gone.

____ ____ ____ ____

It's a Miracle!

(John 2)

There was no wine left at the wedding. Jesus told a servant to fill some jars with water. When the guest of honor tasted the water, it had become wine!

Draw a line to connect the jar halves.

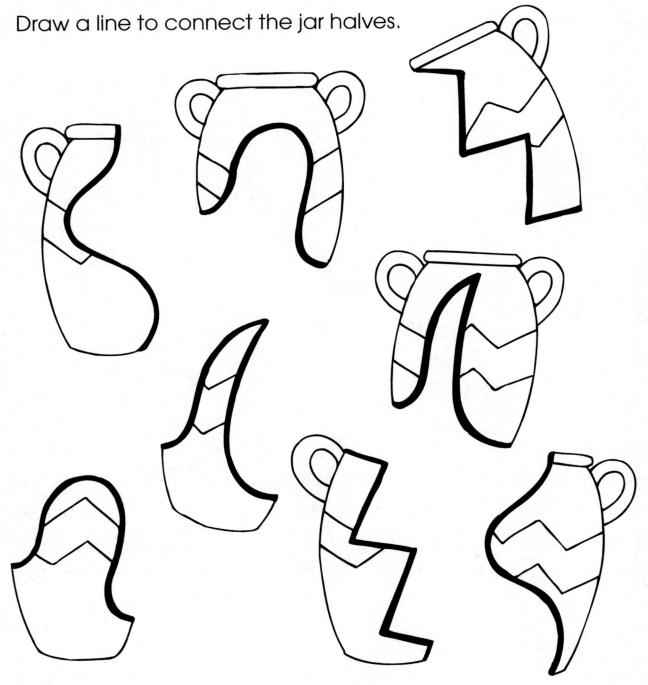

Last but Not Least

(John 2)

The wine Jesus created was delicious. The guest of honor told the groom that he had saved the best for last!

Color the picture using the code.

1 = brown	3 = green	5 = purple	7 = black
2 = orange	4 = red	6 = blue	8 = yellow

The First of Many

(John 2)

The disciples saw that Jesus had the power to turn water into wine. It was the first miracle that Jesus did.

Find the letters that spell **miracle**. Color them blue.

Jesus Calms the Storm

(Matthew 8)

Jesus and the disciples went out on a lake in a small boat.
Jesus was tired and fell asleep.

Put a check by the words that rhyme with **sleep**.

keep ☐	kite ☐	stop ☐
pear ☐	sheep ☐	deep ☐
beep ☐	leap ☐	feet ☐
tire ☐	hand ☐	creep ☐

What a Storm!

(John 2)

While Jesus slept in the boat, a terrible storm started. The waves were high. They started to crash over the boat.

Write these words in the crossword puzzle.

rain

lightning

storm

wind

waves

Help! Jesus, Help!

(Luke 8)

The disciples were terrified that the horrible storm would sink the boat. They were afraid they would drown in the sea. They woke up Jesus. They asked Him to help them.

Count how many times the disciples yelled, "Help." Write that number in the cloud.

Be Still!

(Luke 8)

Jesus told the waves and the wind to be calm. Everything grew quiet. The disciples were amazed at what Jesus did.

Draw in the bottom picture so that it will look like the top one.

A Girl Lives

(Luke 8)

A man named Jairus asked Jesus to come to his house. Someone he loved was very sick. Jairus wanted Jesus to make her well.

To find out who this person was, start at the capital "D" and follow the arrows. Write the letters in order on the blanks.

___ ___ ___ ___ ___ ___ ___ ___ ___

Is It Too Late?

(Luke 8)

Jesus went to Jairus' house. People were crying. They were sad. The sick girl was dead.

Find and color these shapes in the picture below.

Jesus Knows

(Luke 8)

Everyone believed Jairus' daughter was dead. But Jesus said she was not dead. He said she was doing something.

To find out what Jesus said she was doing, write the letter that comes after the one shown. Use the alphabet to help you. Then read the circle from top to bottom to find the answer.

r → ◯

k → ◯

d → ◯

d → ◯

o → ◯

h → ◯

m → ◯

f → ◯

a b c d e f
g h i j k l m
n o p q r s t
u v w x y z

A Happy Day

(Luke 8)

Jesus took hold of the dead girl's hand. He told her to get up. The girl did as Jesus said. She was alive again. How happy her mother and father were!

Use the code to color the picture.

1 - blue	3 - brown	5 - red
2 - green	4 - orange	6 - purple

Fish and Loaves

(Matthew 14)

Jesus and His disciples went to a quiet place. But people found out where Jesus was. They followed Him. Jesus took pity on them. He spoke to them and did something for the sick.

Look down, across, and diagonally for these words.

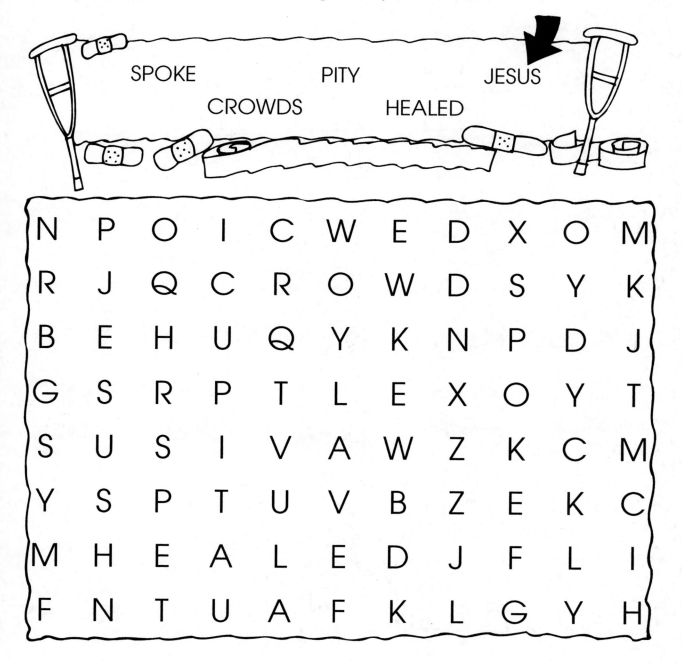

SPOKE   PITY   JESUS

CROWDS   HEALED

N	P	O	I	C	W	E	D	X	O	M
R	J	Q	C	R	O	W	D	S	Y	K
B	E	H	U	Q	Y	K	N	P	D	J
G	S	R	P	T	L	E	X	O	Y	T
S	U	S	I	V	A	W	Z	K	C	M
Y	S	P	T	U	V	B	Z	E	K	C
M	H	E	A	L	E	D	J	F	L	I
F	N	T	U	A	F	K	L	G	Y	H

A Busy Day

(Matthew 14)

It was almost evening. Jesus had been talking and healing people. All day the disciples wanted Him to send the crowds away and let them find food.

Look at each row. Circle the two foods that look alike.

A Little for a Lot

(Matthew 14)

Jesus told His disciples that they could feed the thousands of people that had gathered with them. But the only food available were some loaves of bread and some fish. The disciples wondered how so little could feed so many.

Draw a circle around the basket that has five loaves of bread and two fish.

Food for All

(Matthew 14)

Five loaves of bread and two fish were brought to Jesus.
Jesus thanked God for the food. Then He had the
disciples give the food to the thousands of people.
Through a miracle, Jesus had enough food to feed
everyone! After the people had eaten, there were even
baskets of food left over.

How many baskets do you count? Color that number at
the bottom.

Jesus Walks on Water

(Matthew 14)

The disciples got into a boat and went to a lake called the Sea of Galilee. Jesus stayed behind to pray.

Connect the dots to make a picture.

Windy and Weary

(Matthew 14)

It became very windy on the Sea of Galilee. The disciples' boat was tossed about by the waves. They tried to row towards the shore, but they couldn't.

Find and color these objects: a star, shirt, mitten, heart, and Bible.

A Special Walk

(Matthew 14)

Jesus knew His disciples were in a boat being tossed about by large waves. So He walked out on the water to them. When the disciples saw Him coming, they were frightened!

Write the first letter of each picture to see what they thought Jesus was.

Peter Tries It, Too

(Matthew 14)

As Jesus walked on the water towards his disciples, He told them who He was. He told them not to be afraid. Peter wanted to walk on the water, too. Peter got out of the boat and took some steps. He got scared and began to sink. Jesus held onto him and kept him safe.

Help Jesus and Peter back to the boat.

A Good Samaritan

(Luke 10)

Jesus told a story about a man who was traveling from Jerusalem to Jericho. Along the way, some robbers took his clothes and beat him up.

Fit these words into the crossword puzzle.

traveling   clothes   Jerusalem

robbers   beat   Jericho

Who Will Help?

(Luke 10)

As the man lay hurt, three men passed by. The first was a priest. The second man was a Levite. Finally, a Samaritan came along. He stopped.

Unscramble the letters on the road to find what this man wanted to do.

A Kind Man

(Luke 10)

The Samaritan was the only one who stopped to help the hurt man. He cleaned his wounds and put bandages on them. He brought the injured man to an inn and paid for him to stay there.

Find and color these shapes in the pictures.

Be Kind to Everyone

(Luke 10)

Jesus wanted the people to understand that they should be kind to everyone.

How many hearts do you count in the jumble? Write it in the oval.

Prodigal Son

(Luke 15)

Sometimes Jesus told stories to help people understand things. One day, He told a story about a father with two sons. The youngest son asked his father for money. He took the money and went far away.

Counting by 2's, color the path that will take the son to the sack of money.

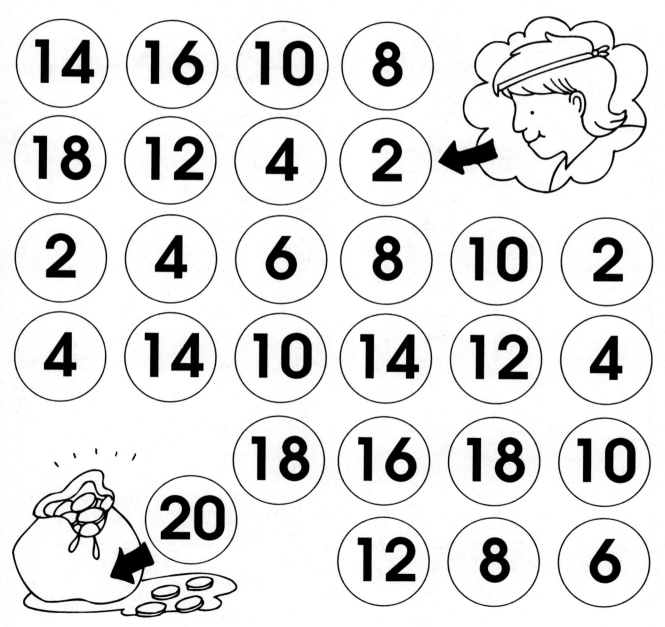

Party Time

(Luke 15)

The son took the money his father gave him and left home. He spent the money in foolish ways. Do you know what happened after awhile?

Use the code to find the answer.

Th___ s___n

b___c___m___

v___r___ p___ ___r!

A Dirty Job

(Luke 15)

The young son had no money. He was hungry. He took a job feeding pigs. The son decided to go home. He hoped his father would give him a job as a servant.

Count each group of pigs. Draw a line from it to the trough with the same number.

A Happy Homecoming

(Luke 15)

When the father saw his son coming down the road, he threw his arms around him. He put a nice robe on his son. He threw a feast for him.

Just like in this story, God loves and welcomes back anyone who has gone away from Him. Use the code to color the picture.

| 1 = blue | 3 = brown | 5 = purple |
| 2 = red | 4 = green | 6 = orange |

Jesus Rides Through Jerusalem

(Mark 11)

The disciples and Jesus were going to Jerusalem. Before they got there, Jesus told two disciples where they would find a certain animal. They found the animal. They took it to Jesus.

To find out what the animal was, use the code to color the picture.

▲ = gray   ■ = blue

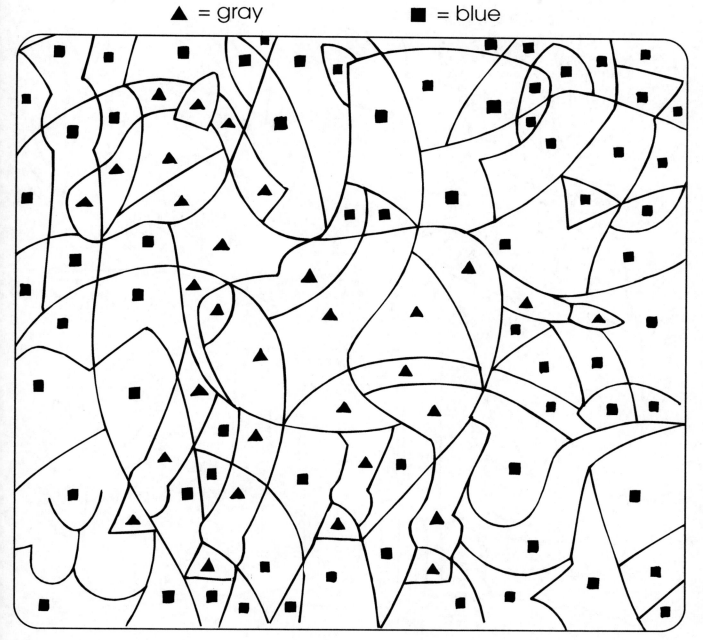

Look Who's Coming

(Mark 11)

The people in Jerusalem laid clothing and palm branches on the road for the donkey and Jesus to walk on. They were so happy. He was coming to their city!

Cross out four palm branches. Next, cross out another two palm branches. When you are finished, count how many palm branches are left. Write that number on the big window of the building.

All Through the Town

(Mark 11)

As Jesus rode the donkey through Jerusalem, people shouted, "Hosanna."

Help Jesus finish His ride through the city.

Jesus Dies and Rises Up

(John 18)

Some people hated Jesus. They planned to do mean things to Him. A crowd of men with weapons and torches came and arrested Jesus in the Garden of Gethsemane.

Match the torch halves together.

He Did Nothing Wrong

(John 18-19)

After Jesus was arrested, He was brought before Pilate, the Roman governor. Pilate said Jesus had done nothing wrong. Even so, the angry people wanted Jesus to be crucified.

Find the same picture of Pilate below.

A Cross to Bear

(John 19)

Jesus was forced to carry a heavy cross to a place called Calvary. Once there, Jesus was nailed to the cross.

Find three hidden crosses below. Color them red.

Accept This Gift

(John 3)

Jesus died on the cross so our sins could be forgiven. He loved us so much that He took our punishment and died in our place. That is why we call Him our "Savior." All you need to do is accept what Jesus did for us and ask God for the forgiveness of our sins. You will then live in heaven with Jesus forever. Will you do this today?

Connect the dots to spell out "Savior."

Jesus Rises Up

(John 20)

After Jesus died on the cross, His body was put inside a tomb. A heavy stone was placed in front of the opening. When Mary Magdalene went to His tomb, she saw that the stone had been rolled away. Jesus was not there!

Find the path that takes Mary to the tomb.

Jesus Is Alive!

(John 20)

At the empty tomb, Mary Magdalene talked to a man. She thought he was a gardener. But then she saw that the man was really Jesus! He had risen from the dead and was alive again!

Color the picture using the code. Cut it out and tape it up so you can be reminded of this wonderful truth!

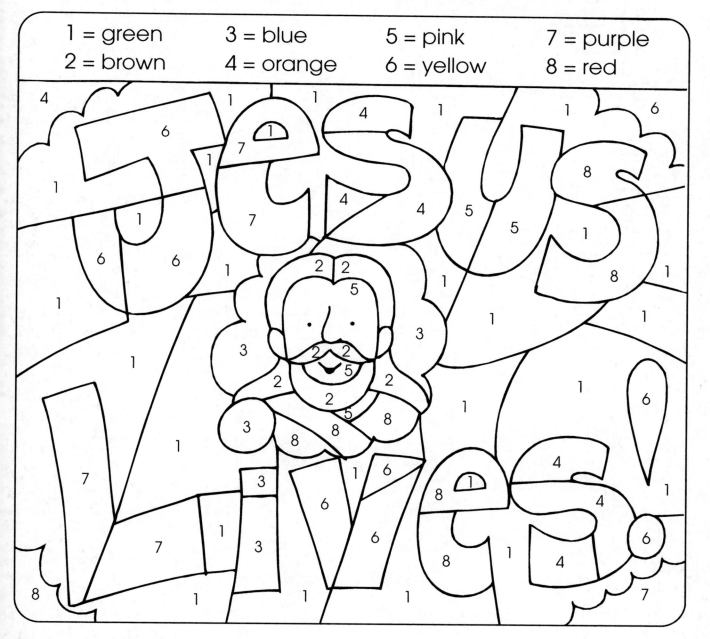

1 = green   3 = blue   5 = pink   7 = purple
2 = brown   4 = orange   6 = yellow   8 = red

Answer Key

(**Note:** Not all pages will have an answer key. Teacher will need to use discretion as needed on coloring pages and various other pages.)

Page 5

11

Page 6

Page 7

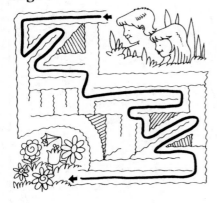

Page 12

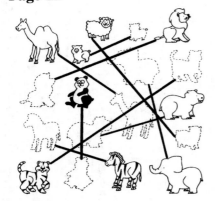

Page 14

rainbow

Page 15

Page 16

Page 18

Answers may vary depending on student's ability to recognize shapes within shapes.

Page 21

B

Page 22

Page 24

They sold him to travelers who took him to Egypt.

Page 25

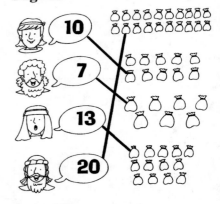

Page 26

forgave

Page 27

SILVER

Page 28

cut

Page 31

NO

Page 32

Page 34

GREAT HAPPINESS

140

Answer Key *(cont.)*

Page 36

3

Page 37

GOAT, NOTE, DOLL

Answer: GOD

Page 38

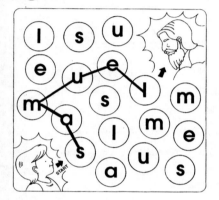

Page 40

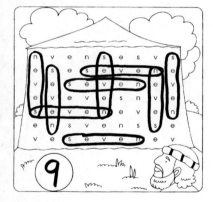

Page 42

middle piece

Page 43

GOLIATH

Page 44

SLINGSHOT

Page 45

slingshot, sword, sun, tree, cloud, helmet point

Page 46

HURRAH

Page 47

Page 49

Page 50

PASSOVER

Page 51

second row, third picture

Page 52

HE WOULDN'T BOW TO HAMAN!

Page 56

second row, second picture

Page 57

Page 59

LOTS OF TROUBLE!

Page 61

9

Page 62

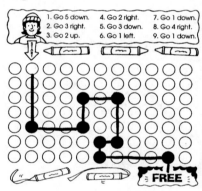

Page 64

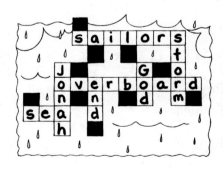

Answer Key *(cont.)*

Page 66

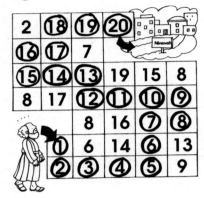

Page 67

2, 5, 7, 9, 10, 13, 14, 17, 20

Page 70

Gabriel

Page 71

Page 72

JUMPED FOR JOY!

Page 74

John

Page 75

Bethlehem

Page 76

7, 12; 13, 6; 9, 16

Page 77

PIG, HEN, COW, CAT

Page 80

AFRAID

Page 81

11

Page 82

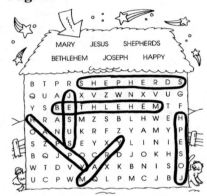

Page 83

Page 85

blessed

Page 86

SAVIOR

Page 88

HARM JESUS

Page 89

Page 91

first row: first cake and third cake

second row: second cake

fourth row: second cake

Page 92

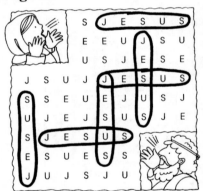

Page 93

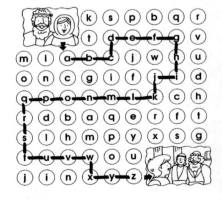

Page 94

HIS FATHER'S HOUSE

142

Answer Key *(cont.)*

Page 95

WILD HONEY

Page 96

JORDAN

Page 99

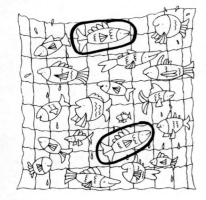

Page 100

From now on you will catch men.

Page 101

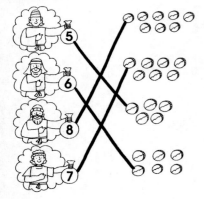

Page 102

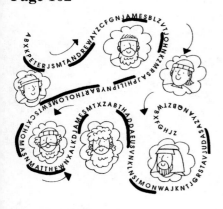

Page 103

WINE

Page 104

Page 107

keep, sheep, deep, beep, leap, creep

Page 108

Page 109

14

Page 111

Daughter

Page 113

sleeping

Page 115

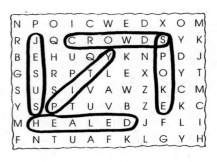

Page 116

Page 117

second row: third picture

Page 118

12

Page 121

ghost

Page 122

         #7100 Bible Brain Teasers

Bible Brain Teasers

Answer Key *(cont.)*

Page 123

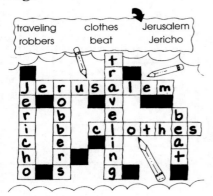

Page 124

HELP HIM!

Page 126

15

Page 127

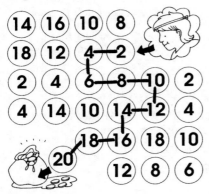

Page 128

The son became very poor!

Page 129

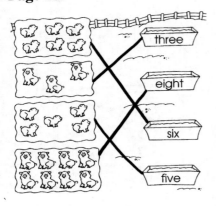

Page 132

3

Page 133

Page 134

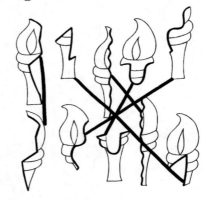

Page 135

picture on the bottom right

Page 138

Joseph and the Colorful Coat

(Genesis 37)

Jacob had twelve sons. His favorite son was Joseph. One day, Jacob gave Joseph a special gift.

Connect the dots to find out what this gift was. Color it with lots of different colors.

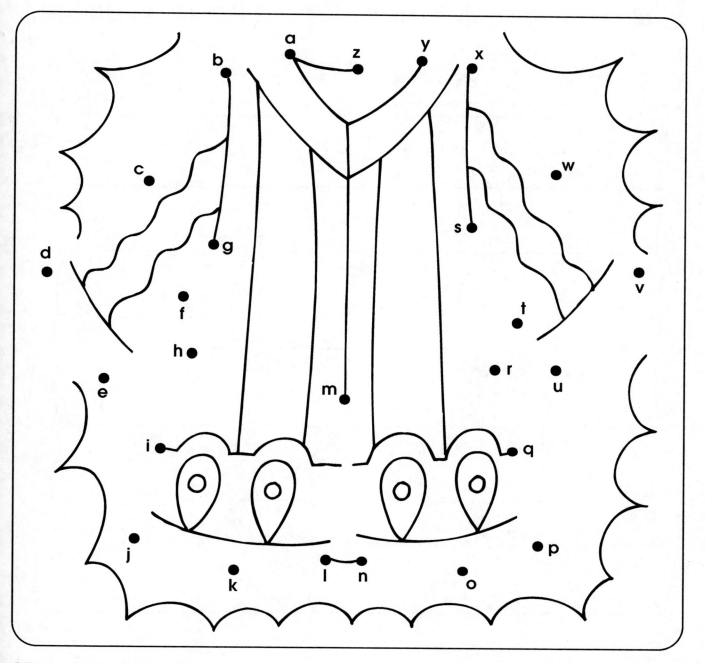

Angry Brothers

(Genesis 37)

Joseph's brothers were angry that Joseph got a new coat. They thought their father loved Joseph more than them.

Use the shape code to fill in the missing letters. It will tell you what the brothers did to Joseph.

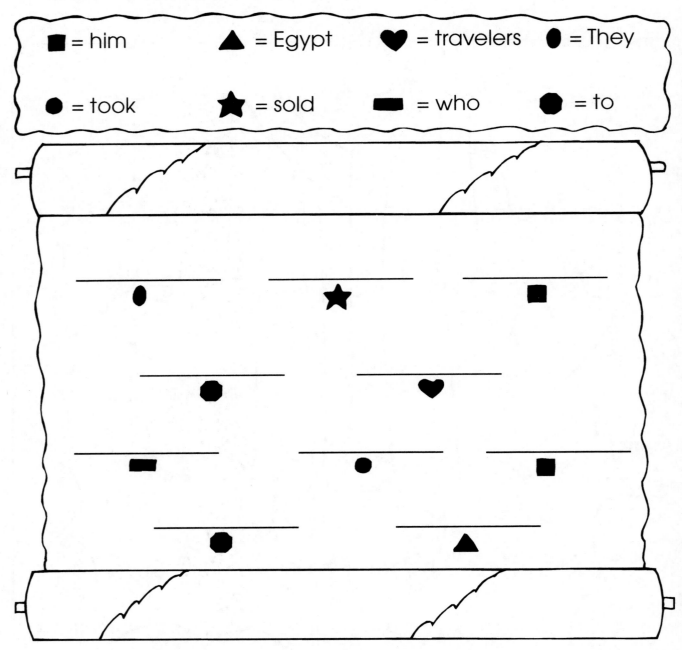

Hungry Brothers

(Genesis 41–42)

The Pharaoh of Egypt gave Joseph an important job. Many years later, Joseph saw his brothers when they came to Egypt to get food. Joseph's brothers didn't recognize him.

Draw a line from each brother to the number of sacks of food he is asking for.

Joseph Is Kind

(Genesis 45)

Joseph told the men that he was their brother. Joseph could have been angry at his brothers because they had treated him badly, but he was not.

Write the first letter of each picture to find out what Joseph did.

Naomi and Ruth

(Ruth 1)

Ruth's husband died. Ruth's mother-in-law, Naomi, told Ruth to go away and start a new life. To find out what Ruth said, color the shapes using the code.

1, 2, 3 = red   4, 5, 6 = yellow

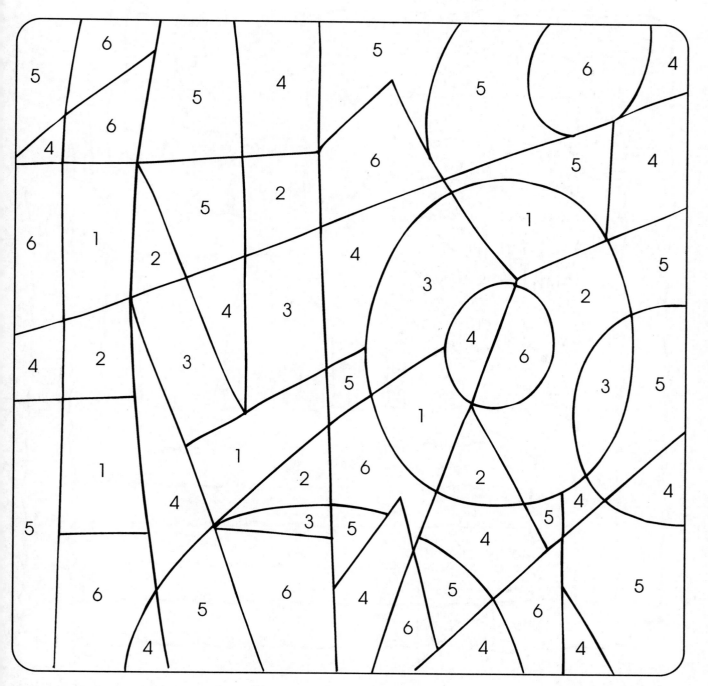

Working for Food

(Ruth 1–2)

Ruth and her mother-in-law went to Bethlehem. It was harvest time.

Help Ruth through the field so she can pick up the leftover barley.

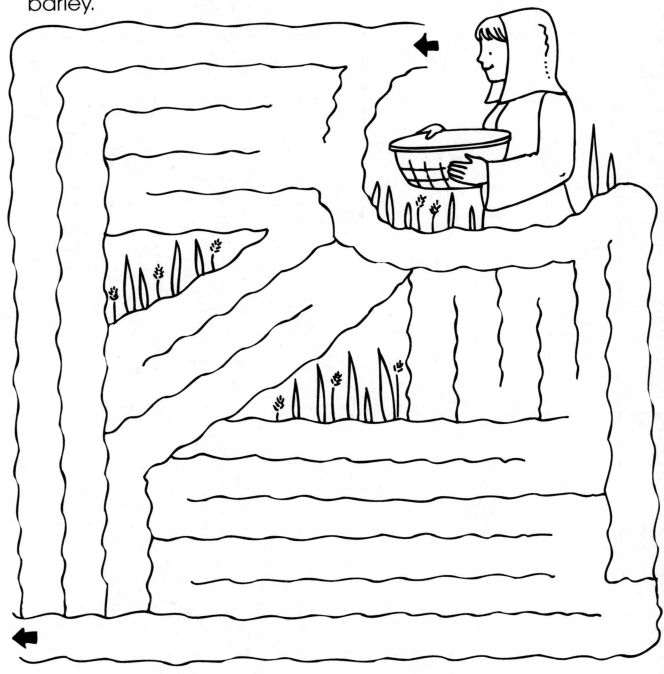

A Nice Couple

(Ruth 2 and 4)

Boaz was the owner of the fields in which Ruth collected barley. Boaz learned how kind Ruth was to Naomi. Soon Boaz and Ruth got married.

Finish drawing each flower for the wedding.

Grandma Naomi

(Ruth 4)

After Ruth and Boaz married, they had a baby.

Use the code to find what this little boy brought to Naomi.

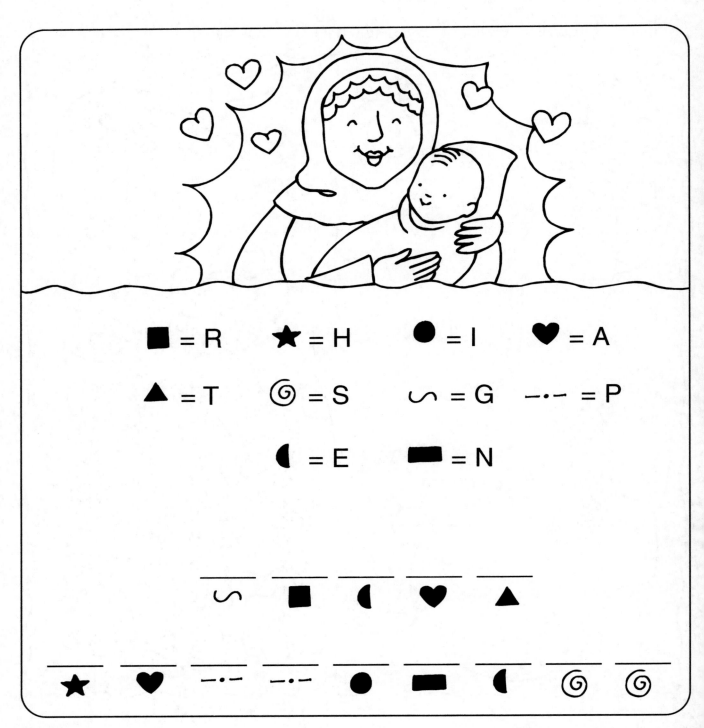

Josiah Listens to God

(2 Kings 23)

King Josiah wanted to obey God. He had all the statues and all the false gods destroyed.

Match the halves together.

Time to Celebrate!

(2 Kings 23)

To please God, King Josiah burned all the statues of false gods. Then Josiah's kingdom celebrated something special.

Color only the capital letters on the balloons. Then write the letters in order on the blanks to find the answer.

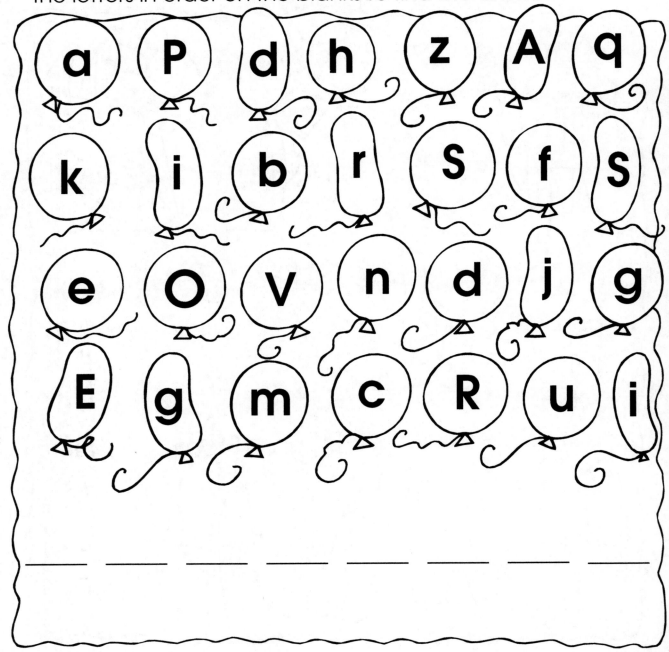

_____ _____ _____ _____ _____ _____ _____ _____ _____ _____

Jonah and the Big Fish

(Jonah 1)

God told the prophet Jonah to go to the city of Nineveh. God wanted Jonah to tell the people to stop being bad. Jonah didn't want to go. Instead, he got on a ship to go somewhere else.

Finish all the ships so they look like the top one.

A Super Storm

(Jonah 1)

While Jonah sailed at sea, God sent a terrible storm. Jonah told the sailors that God was angry at him for running away. Jonah told the sailors to toss him overboard and the storm would end.

Write these words in the crossword puzzle.

| overboard | end | God | sailors |
| Jonah | sea | storm | |

Jesus Is Baptized

(Matthew 3)

John the Baptist lived in the desert. He wore camel's hair clothing and a belt made of leather.

Unscramble the letters in the cactus plants to find out what John ate.

Confess and Be Baptized

(Matthew 3)

People came to hear John the Baptist preach. After they admitted their sins, John would baptize them in a river.

To find the river's name, write only the capital letters in order in the blank.

Please Baptize Me

(Matthew 3)

Jesus wanted John to baptize Him. John didn't think he was worthy enough to do this. When Jesus asked him again, John baptized Jesus.

Find and color seven hidden frogs green in the picture.

God Loves His Son

(Matthew 3)

Right after John baptized Jesus, something appeared in the sky. God said He was pleased with His beloved son.

Connect the dots to create what appeared in the sky.